P9-CAO-932

I Want Our Love to Last Forever

...and I Know It Can If We Both Want It To

Other Bestselling Books by Blue Mountain Press

Books by Susan Polis Schutz:
To My Daughter, with Love, on the Important Things in Life
To My Son with Love
Love, Love, Love

For You, Just Because You're Very Special to Me
by Collin McCarty

100 Things to Always Remember... and One Thing to Never Forget
by Alin Austin

Anthologies:
42 Gifts I'd Like to Give to You
A Sister Is a Very Special Friend
Be Proud of All You've Achieved
The Best Thing in Life Is a Friend
Creeds to Live By, Dreams to Follow
Don't Ever Give Up Your Dreams
For a Special Teenager
For You, My Daughter
I Keep Falling in Love with You
I Want Our Love to Last Forever
Life Can Be Hard Sometimes... but It's Going to Be Okay
Marriage Is a Promise of Love
Mother, I Love You
Mother, Thank You for All Your Love
Mottos to Live By
Reach Out for Your Dreams
Take Each Day One Step at a Time
There Is Greatness Within You, My Son
Thoughts of Love
True Friends Always Remain in Each Other's Heart

Blue Mountain Press®

Boulder, Colorado

I Want
Our Love
to Last Forever

...and I Know It Can
If We Both Want It To

A collection of poems
from Blue Mountain Arts®

Blue Mountain Press ®

Boulder, Colorado

Copyright © 1994 by Stephen Schutz and Susan Polis Schutz.
Copyright © 1994 by Blue Mountain Arts, Inc.

All rights reserved. No part of this book may be reproduced in any
manner whatsoever without written permission from the publisher.

Library of Congress Catalog Card Number: 94-6250
ISBN: 0-88396-375-2

ACKNOWLEDGMENTS appear on page 62.

Ħ design on book cover is registered in
U.S. Patent and Trademark Office.

Manufactured in the United States of America
First Printing: March, 1994

Library of Congress Cataloging-in-Publication Data

I want our love to last forever—and I know it can if we both want it
   to : a collection of poems from Blue Mountain Arts.
      p.   cm.
   ISBN 0-88396-375-2 : $7.95
   1. Love poetry, American. 2. American poetry—20th century.
I. Blue Mountain Arts (Firm)
PS595.L6I15   1994
811'.54080354—dc20   94-6250
                                                         CIP

Blue Mountain Press ®

P.O. Box 4549, Boulder, Colorado 80306

CONTENTS

Our Love Will Always See Us Through the Difficult Times

Relationships aren't always easy.
We have faced so many problems
and struggled so many times.
And yet, even when things are
at their worst,
I think of what we have,
and I know that
no matter how tough
things may become,
our relationship is worth
the effort it may take
to face anything life
brings our way.

I believe that we have found
a once-in-a-lifetime love
and a relationship worth
a lifetime of devotion.
And if we try —
if we hold on a little tighter
and pull together
a little harder—
we can keep what we have
and we can face anything together.
Relationships aren't always easy,
but ours is worth whatever it takes,
and our love will see us through.

— Deanne Laura Gilbert

Our Love
Can Last Forever
If We Both Want It To

I want to have
a lasting relationship
with you
I know that this will mean that
we both must work hard
   to please each other
   to help each other
   to be fair and honest with each other
   to accept each other as we really are

Our love can last forever
if we want it to
We both must work hard
   to keep our individuality
      yet also become one with each other
   to remain strong and supportive of each other
      in adverse times as well as in good times
   to be exciting and interesting
      to ourselves and to each other

We both must work hard
to always consider each other
the most important person in the world
to always consider love
the most important emotion
that we can feel
to always consider our relationship
the most serious and significant
union of two people

Even though it may not always be easy
to have a lasting relationship
working hard is very easy
when the results can be
the beauty of a loving and lasting
us
I love you

—Susan Polis Schutz

Let's Be Patient
with Each Other

Most relationships go through
  stressful times.
And that is why it is so important
when one of us is having
  a difficult time
to step back and realize
that what we may do or say
should not be taken personally.
If you need to draw away,
I need to remember
that it is your sorting time
  and not a rejection of me.
And when I am quiet,
it does not mean I don't want
  to be with you.
It is just that I am thinking
  things through.

Let us always be patient
  with each other
and recognize and respect
  each other's individual needs.
Because if we each have
  our own inner strength,
our relationship will be stronger
and better able to withstand
  difficult times.

—Charlene A. Forsten

These Are the Keys
to a Loving, Lasting Relationship

—*Enjoy!*
—*Love one another with all your heart.*
—*Give more than you take.*
—*Don't ever take your relationship for granted.*
—*Have heart-to-heart talks and really communicate.*
—*Be trusting, playful, intimate, and kind.*
—*Appreciate all the little, special things.*
—*Recognize that time spent together is a treasure.*
—*Make the most of what each day brings.*
—*Know that nothing is sweeter than the warmth of one hand holding another.*
—*Walk together in the direction you both want to go.*
—*Be supportive and open to changes.*
—*Always continue to grow.*

—Cherish this blessing that so few truly find.
—Have dreams to reach out for through the years.
—Share one another's smiles through the good times.
—Be everything to one another through the tears.
—What your time together lacks in quantity,
   make up for with quality.
—Call to say "I love you" in the middle of the day.
—Keep your sense of humor and hold on to your
   hopes.
—Don't let work or worries get in the way.
—Make love a sanctuary and a celebration.
—Make each moment more precious than the one
   before.
—Realize how lucky you are to be two...together.
—And make the best memories any two people
   ever had.

—Casey Whilson

Getting Through the Hard Times
Is Part of What Love Is All About

Do you remember when we first met?
Do you remember how close we were,
and how much we loved being together?
It was as if we could conquer the world—
just the two of us.

I wish sometimes that we could
feel that way more often.
We seem to have drifted apart.
So much has happened to us since we first met.
Our lives were simple back then;
now we have many responsibilities.

We've been through a lot of changes.
Yet one thing has never changed—
my love for you.
Somehow everything else doesn't seem
as overwhelming as long as you're here
changing and growing with me.

So even in these times when things seem harder,
I think we can take comfort in knowing
that we'll make it with the help of
that very same love that brought us together
not so very long ago.

—Jennifer Nelson-Fenwick

To Love Someone
Is Life's Greatest Gift

To love someone
is to experience every other emotion
outside of love and still come back
to love.

To love someone
is to feel hurt or pain, and be
able to overcome it and to forget
about it.

To love someone
is to realize that the other
person is not perfect. It is
being able to see their bad parts,
but put emphasis on the parts you
love, and gladly accept them for
the individual they are.

To love someone
is to lay a strong base for your
feelings, but leave room for some
fluctuation, because to feel
exactly the same way all the time
would leave no room for growth,
experience, and learning.

To love someone
is to be strong at accepting new
ideas and facts. It is knowing
that a person will not stay the
same, but also that change
happens gradually.

To love someone
    is to give until your heart aches.
    The greatest gifts shared between
    two people are trust and
    understanding, which come from
    love. Love is giving one hundred
    and ten percent of yourself and
    only wanting something as simple
    as a smile in return.

To love someone
    is to be able to see not only
    with your eyes but with your
    heart. It is to develop insight into
    your feelings and the other person's
    feelings, and to have a good
    understanding of your relationship.

To love someone
    is to give of yourself totally,
    saying, "Here I am, and all
    that I am loves you very much."
    It is not twisting and turning and
    changing yourself to gain approval,
    but it is improving yourself so
    that your good points catch the
    other's attention and overshadow
    your faults.

—Teresa M. Reiches

No one is perfect
therefore no relationship can be perfect
So please don't get
discouraged or disillusioned with us
when things go astray
What is important
is that our love will never go astray
because I love and appreciate you so much
As we continue to grow
and change as individuals
our relationship will continue
to grow and change as well
But since at the core of our relationship
there is a very deep respect and love
for one another
our love can only grow stronger
and more beautiful every day

—Susan Polis Schutz

I Need to Be Able
to Share
My Feelings with You

*There are times when I think
that the best thing I can do
    for you — and for us —
is to tell you how I feel.
This may not seem like much to you,
    but it is very important to me.*

*If it's truly how I feel,
it doesn't matter
if the words are new or old.
What matters is sharing them with you.
If it's truly how I feel,
it doesn't matter if the words
    are happy or sad,
        angry or loving.
What matters is sharing them with you.*

*When I tell you how I feel,
we're each at a better place
and able to come together
on common ground.
So often my feelings mirror yours,
but when they don't,
    it's even more important
to talk things through.
The words aren't always easy to say,
but what matters most
    is sharing them with you.*

—Linda Sackett-Morrison

Communication Is the Greatest Power We Possess

Communication is the link
between all creation—
the bridge that carries
our messages and ideas
across the rivers of silence.
Without it, we are left alone
with our own assumptions
and misconceived ideas of reality.
Communication is a source of power
in relationships—
a strength that allows personalities
to express themselves.
Communication is the only way
in which the truth can be told,
whether it be written or spoken.
Without communication,
life would be restricted
by a series of unanswered questions, and
an endless chain of misunderstood events
would dominate our world.
Communication is the greatest
power we possess;
it should be valued and used
to its fullest extent.

—Kelly D. Caron

No Matter What Dark Clouds
May Come Our Way,
Let's Keep On Shining like the Sun

We both know that
no matter how many clouds
get in the way,
the sun keeps on shining.
No matter how many times its rays
are blocked from our view,
the sun will reappear
  on another day
to shine more brilliantly
  than before.

It takes determination
to outlast those dark clouds
that sometimes enter our life together,
and patience to keep on shining
no matter what gets in our way.
But it will all pay off eventually,
because our love and the sun
have a lot in common:
they're both going to shine
no matter what.

—Barbara J. Hall

We're a Perfect Example
of How Opposites Attract

When I say "yes," you contemplate "no."
When I think of solving a problem one way,
   you have an entirely different approach.
We are compatible, though at times combustible.
We can be the best of friends
   or the worst of enemies.
We can comfort and care for each other,
   and then without even thinking,
   we can be callous and neglectful.
We can be cruel and kind and a thousand
   other combinations of emotions.

We have different moods at different times
and distinct ways of dealing with our lives.
But deep down inside,
we have a very special feeling of love
   for each other that will keep us close
during all of our ups, downs, and
   the other crazy, opposite situations
      we get ourselves into.

—Ben Daniels

I'm Sorry for the Times
When I Get Angry

I'm sorry for those times
when I'm not who I should be,
when I grow impatient
and frustrated
because things don't work out.
I know that you, too,
have things on your mind,
and I have no right
   to become upset with you.
It's just hard sometimes
   to understand
   the way things go wrong,
and I wanted you to know
that I'm sorry for those times
   when I become harsh
   and angry with you.
I hope you can understand
   and forgive me.

—Bethanie Jean Brevik

Will You Meet Me Halfway?

Will you meet me halfway

on the road back to understanding
as we try to overcome the tension
and the silence?

As we recall all that we were in better days
gone by.

As we try to capture all those loving feelings
that seem so distant now.

As we try once more to cement
the bond of our love
so fragile and so young.

As we try one more time to heal our pain
and disappointment.

I will meet you more than halfway,
if you will meet me halfway.

—Tim Connor

Some Advice on
How to Resolve Arguments

Whenever we become involved
   in a confrontation,
it's best to allow ourselves
some time to really think about
all sides of the situation.
Before becoming defensive,
let's give ourselves the opportunity
   to be receptive.
All problems have more than
   one answer;
there are always
   extenuating circumstances
for each of us to consider.

We must be willing to listen
and be open to the possibility
that things can be worked out,
that nothing has such an
   all-encompassing conclusion
that we cannot reach a compromise.
Before we enter into
   a major debate,
let's take time to compose our thoughts
   and feelings.
We need to realize that anything
   and everything in life
has its own unique perspective,
and before we jump to any conclusions,
it's important to allow ourselves
the time to completely understand.

—Deanna Beisser

I Thank You Deeply for Being the Person Whom I Love

It seems like the more I love you
the more sensitive I become
I find myself becoming hurt too easily
and for no reason at all
Sometimes you do something completely normal
but it might not include me
and I feel so slighted
I appear cold to you
but really I am just hurt
Please bear with me during these times
and understand that I am not trying
to put pressure on you
It is just that my love for you
has made me extremely vulnerable
and though I don't like feeling hurt so easily
love has opened up for me
a new sense of awareness
of myself and of other people
I thank you deeply for bringing out
the new depths of emotions
that I now feel
and I thank you deeply for
being the person whom all
these beautiful and intense
feelings of love
are for

—Susan Polis Schutz

As Much As I Love You,
I Still Need to Be Alone Sometimes

Sometimes I just need
   a little space to myself:
a little room to breathe,
   a time set apart just for me.
It isn't that I don't love you,
   because I do.
Sometimes I just need
   to be alone for a while,
so I can recharge myself
   and become a better person.
It is no reflection on you
   or on our love;
it's just that some solitude
   is necessary for me.

Sometimes I just need
   to sit back and relax,
taking in all the things
   that are happening in my world,
and sorting through
   my feelings and thoughts.
Taking some time for myself
   is as vital to me as breathing;
it keeps me going when stresses come.

Sometimes I just need to pull back,
   to stand apart,
to focus on what is urgent.
It is at these times
   that I most need you
      and your understanding.
It is then that I need
   a friend as well as a lover.

At these times, please know
   that I still love you,
I still care,
   and I want you to be happy.
It is just that I cannot
   love you the right way
unless I love and take care
   of myself, too.

—Donna Reames

*Love takes time. It needs a history
of giving and receiving, laughing
and crying.
Love involves much careful and active
listening. It is doing whatever needs to
be done, and embracing whatever will
promote the other's happiness, security,
and well-being. Sometimes, love hurts.
Love realizes and accepts that there will be
disagreements and disturbing emotions...
There may be times when miles lay between,
but love is a commitment. It believes,
and endures all things.*

—Barb Upham

*Let's work slowly with each
other and build a relationship
that we both can enjoy being
a part of.*

*Let's share love and understand
that neither of us is perfect;
we are both subject to human
frailties.*

*Let's encourage each other
to pursue our dreams, even
when we're weary from trying.*

*Let's expect the best that
we both have to give
and still love when we fall
short of our expectations.*

*Let's be friends and respect
each other's individual personality
and give one another room to grow.*

*Let's be candid with each other
and point out strengths and
weaknesses.*

*Let's understand each other's
personal philosophy,
even if we don't agree.*

Let's be friends as well as lovers.

—Denise Braxton-Brown

I Know We Can Make It

I have never wanted anything
like I want
  my loveliest hopes
   of you and me
    to come true.

I can picture us
  years from now,
happier than ever,
sharing so much understanding,
growing together,

  being together,

   and staying together.

My hopes and dreams know that
we can make it if we try.

  And so do I.

— Carle Jordan

Together We Can Achieve
a Lifetime of Happiness

*Together we share the joy of a
deep commitment and a sacred trust.
We have given each other
the most precious gift of love.
Let's treasure it, nurture it,
and encourage it
with all the honesty
we used in creating it.
We are sharing something
rare and beautiful.
Let's always speak the truth
and listen attentively,
so that we may understand
each other's thoughts and intentions.
Let's inspire each other
by sharing our accomplishments.
Let's say "I love you" often
to retain the warmth between us.
Let's laugh a lot, too.
Even when we're angry,
let's remember we're
each other's best friend.
Let's stand together
and for each other always;
let's be content in mind and spirit.
Let's make each day a blessing
and a fulfillment of our dreams.*

—William Scott Galasso

We're Two Different People, and Let's Not Try to Change That!

Instead of minimizing our differences
let us maximize them
Instead of denying that you are better at this
and I am better at that
let us take full advantage of our special skills
and recognize the weaknesses
in order either to work on them
or to turn to what we do best
It is okay with me
that most men have better spatial skills
and that most women are better at verbal skills
I can accept that most men are more concerned
*   with objects*
and most women with people
That boys excel at gross motor coordination
and girls at manual dexterity
That males are good at problem solving
and females process information faster
I like our differences!
As you shovel the driveway
I fix you hot soup
As you drive at night
I keep you awake
As you carry the suitcases
I check in at the counter

You figure our taxes
I decide on our budget
You vacuum
I dust
You turn the mattress over
I water the plants
You chop the onions
I add the spices
You go shopping
but with my list
You buy me books
I buy you shirts
You know how to cure the ills of the world
I know how to cure your ills
You know what the children ought to do
I know how they are
You know about driving in the snow
I know you should wear a scarf
You show me how much you love me
I tell it to you
I could not do well what you do so well
nor could you do what I do
I like me as me
and you as you.

—Natasha Josefowitz

If I Sometimes
Hold On to You
Too Tightly...

It Is Only Because
I Love You So Much

*If I want to take up a lot of your time,
it is because your presence
gives me so much pleasure.*

*If I worry about you too much,
it is my own fear
of losing the one I truly love.*

*If I don't want to share you
with anyone else,
it is because my heart wants
to be with only you.*

*If my eyes see only you,
and my heart holds room for
no one else...
It is only because I love you
so much.*

— *Nancy A. Prunty*

I Wish We Could
Spend More Time Together—
Just the Two of Us

The times we spend alone with each other
are so important to me,
and when we don't have those times,
there's a feeling of loneliness
that seems to touch
every part of my life.

You are the only one that
I always want to be with
and whom I never tire of.
The time we take just for us
always adds a new dimension to our love
and strengthens the closeness between us
that I treasure.
Without our special times,
my life seems like an empty shell
and my heart is a weak and lonely place.

I love being with you,
and I never want to be without
everything we share.

—Linda Sackett-Morrison

Sometimes I Just Need
to Hear You Say, "I Care"

When you say, "I care," it means
that you will always do everything
you can to understand.
It means that you will never hurt me.
It means that I can trust you.
It means that I can tell you
what's wrong.
It means that you will try to fix what you can,
that you will listen
when I need you to hear, and that—
even in my most difficult moment—
all I have to do is say the word,
and your hand and my hand
will not be apart.

It means that whenever I speak to you,
whether words are spoken through a smile
or through a tear...
you will listen with your heart.

—Chris Gallatin

Seems like after all we've been through
We would have learned by now
Never to fight for who gets the last word
It doesn't matter anyhow

But around and around we go in circles
Trying to work things through
And sometimes it feels like miles
*   between us...*
But I love you so much that in spite
*   of the struggle*
I keep coming back to you

— Beth Nielsen Chapman and Bill Lloyd,
  from the song, "I Keep Coming Back to You"

It Isn't Always Easy
to Be in a Relationship

*...but there's no place I'd rather be
than in love with you*

*It's not always easy
to be what we want to be for one another.
Sometimes it's difficult to keep our relationship
growing and moving in new directions,
instead of feeling too much the same,
day after day.
Sometimes we struggle for an understanding
of one another's feelings; of what it means
to be in a relationship; of how to find
some kind of fulfillment as individuals;
and of how to bring ourselves together
to make one better union.*

It isn't always easy.

But what matters to me
* is that we're trying.*
Sure, we have questions.
But I can't tell you how much it means
* when we search for the answers...together.*
To my way of thinking, that's the second
* most important thing we can do.*

* The first is for you to keep on*
*   believing in me,*
*   the way that I will always*
*   believe in you.*

That's how love works.
* And I do love you.*

—Alin Austin

*B*eginning today,
I'm going to hug you more often,
I'm going to kiss you more often,
I'm going to touch you more often,
I'm going to talk with you more often.

Beginning today,
most of all,
I'm going to tell you more often
how very much
I love you.

—Beth Fagan Quinn

I Never Want to Change You

Sometimes I think of you
as a part of me,
and I forget that you are
a unique individual
with your own past and future.
Though I want to be in your life,
I realize that I can only be
a part of it, not all of it.

I know you have your own memories
and feelings
that make you who you are,
and in trying to change them,
I'd be changing you.
And though there are things
we need to work on,
I want you to know
that I fell in love with you
just the way you are.

Though sometimes it may seem
like I want to run your life
or change you
or have you do things my way,
ultimately what I want is for you
to be true to yourself.
I want you to feel free
to be an individual;
I want you to want to share your life
with me.

—Barbara Cage

All I Want
Is to Love You Always

*I know it's hard for you sometimes
to understand how I really feel.
At times, I can be the most
lovable person for you to be around;
at other times, it may seem
as though I don't care.
But if you look deep down
inside of my heart,
you'll see that all I want is to
love and care for you forever.
Through happiness and heartbreaks,
you'll always be my life,
my hope, and my inspiration
for all that I achieve.
Through all of my life's journeys,
I'll always love you.*

—Rhett D. Kimble

An Affirmation for
a Loving, Lasting Relationship

I don't expect perfection from you,
for I respect who you are,
and I don't expect you not to fail sometimes,
for you are just as human as I am.
I don't seek to know all your secrets,
for I know that you are an individual,
and I don't ask that you fill all my needs,
for I understand that you have hopes
and dreams of your own.
I don't question your strength,
for I know how far you've come,
and I don't expect you to
carry every burden alone,
for I am here
to go through it all with you.
I don't ask that you possess all the answers,
for I know there will be times
when you're as unsure as I am.
I only ask that you let me be your friend
when you need strength or laughter,
your partner when it comes to our dreams
and our future,
your comfort when you need to forget
the world outside,
and always I ask that you remember
how much I love you.

—Jennifer Nelson-Fenwick

The Commitment
to Love

Love is the strongest and
most fulfilling emotion possible
It lets you share
your goals, your desires, your experiences
It lets you share
your life with someone
It lets you be yourself
    with someone who will always support you
It lets you speak
your innermost feelings
    to someone who understands you
It lets you feel tenderness and warmth—
    a wholeness that avoids loneliness
Love lets you feel complete

But in order to have
a successful love relationship
you must make a strong commitment to each other and love
and you must do and feel everything within your mind and body
    to make this commitment work

You must be happy with yourself
    and you must understand yourself
before you can expect someone else
to be happy with you or to understand you
You must be honest about yourself and each other at all times
    and not hold any feelings back
You must accept each other the way you are
    and not try to change each other
You must be free to grow as individuals yet share your life as one
    but not live your life through each other
You must follow your own principles and morals
    and not follow what society tells you to do
You must follow the philosophy that men and women are equal
    and not treat either person with inferiority in any way

In order to have
a successful love relationship
you must be together always in your heart
    but not necessarily always in your activities
You must be proud of each other and love
    and not be ashamed to show your sensitive feelings
You must treat every day spent with each other as special
    and not take each other or your love for granted
You must spend time talking with each other every day
    and not be too busy with outside events that you
    are too tired for each other
You must understand each other's moods and feelings
    and not hurt each other intentionally
    but if your frustrations are taken out on each other
    you must both realize that it is not a personal attack
You must be passionate with each other often
    and not get into boring patterns
You must continue to have fun and excitement with each other
    and not be afraid to try new things
You must always work at love and your love relationship
    and not forget how important this relationship is
    or what you would feel like without it

Love is the strongest
and most fulfilling emotion possible
If you live your commitment to love
you will live your dreams
between awakenings

—Susan Polis Schutz

I'll Never Love Anyone
the Way I Love You

In loving you, I have experienced
the happiness, the hurt,
the feeling of forever,
the need to be with you and love you.
It's all here inside of me.
It's you I always think about,
it's you I always miss,
and it will always be you,
because you are the one I love.
To me, love means forever.
No one will ever take your place
or know me as you do.
You always know what I'm thinking
and what I'm feeling deep down.
I'll never love anyone
the way I love you.

—Geralynne Dodgen

Working Things Out Between Us

We're going to be okay, you and I.

Everybody goes through some rough times
   once in a while. And, though it's hard
to keep in perspective right now...
it's those times that make people grow
and become stronger.

Lessons get learned.
The one that is most important
is all based on communication.
On being able to open up and talk to
   each other.
About anything and everything. Turning to
one another when a problem arises; not
   turning away.

*Another lesson is that changes aren't
necessarily bad; sometimes they can be
for the best. What's important is learning
how to deal with the inevitable changes that
come to all people in the days of their lives.*

*With patience and trust, and the love that has
been intertwined with our lives for so long,
  we can be strong. We can talk,
and in the course of our discussion,
  probably learn things about
one another we never knew before.*

We can turn to one another and not turn away.

  *We can work things out.
    And we're going to be okay.*

—Chris Gallatin

ACKNOWLEDGMENTS

The following is a partial list of authors and authors' representatives whom the publisher especially wishes to thank for permission to reprint their works.

Linda Sackett-Morrison for "I Need to Be Able to Share My Feelings with You" and "I Wish We Could Spend More Time Together — Just the Two of Us." Copyright © 1994 by Linda Sackett-Morrison. All rights reserved. Reprinted by permission.

Kelly D. Caron for "Communication Is the Greatest Power We Possess." Copyright © 1994 by Kelly D. Caron. All rights reserved. Reprinted by permission.

Ben Daniels for "We're a Perfect Example of How Opposites Attract." Copyright © 1994 by Ben Daniels. All rights reserved. Reprinted by permission.

Tim Connor for "Will You Meet Me Halfway?" From **Walk Easy with Me Through Life** by Tim Connor. Copyright © 1992 by Tim Connor. All rights reserved. Reprinted by permission.

Deanna Beisser for "Some Advice on How to Resolve Arguments." Copyright © 1994 by Deanna Beisser. All rights reserved. Reprinted by permission.

Donna Reames for "As Much as I Love You, I Still Need to Be Alone Sometimes." Copyright © 1994 by Donna Reames. All rights reserved. Reprinted by permission.

Natasha Josefowitz for "We're Two Different People, and Let's Not Try to Change That!" From **Is This Where I Was Going?** by Natasha Josefowitz, published by Warner Books. Copyright © 1983 by Natasha Josefowitz. All rights reserved. Reprinted by permission.

Beth Nielsen Chapman and Bill Lloyd for "Seems like after all we've been through...." Copyright © 1990 by BMG Songs, Inc. and Careers—BMG Music Publishing, Inc. All rights reserved. Used by permission.

Barbara Cage for "I Never Want to Change You." Copyright © 1994 by Barbara Cage. All rights reserved. Reprinted by permission.

A careful effort has been made to trace the ownership of poems used in this anthology in order to obtain permission to reprint copyrighted materials and give proper credit to the copyright owners. If any error or omission has occurred, it is completely inadvertent, and we would like to make corrections in future editions provided that written notification is made to the publisher:

BLUE MOUNTAIN PRESS, INC., P.O. Box 4549, Boulder, Colorado 80306.

This book is printed on fine quality, laid embossed, 80 lb. paper. This paper has been specially produced to be acid free (neutral pH) and contains no groundwood or unbleached pulp. It conforms with all of the requirements of the American National Standards Institute, Inc., so as to ensure that this book will last and be enjoyed by future generations.